THE ELECTORAL COLLEGE

A Kid's Guide

by Cari Meister

CAPSTONE PRESS
a capstone imprint

Captivate is published by Capstone Press, an imprint of Capstone.
1710 Roe Crest Drive, North Mankato, Minnesota 56003
www.capstonepub.com

Copyright © 2020 by Capstone. All rights reserved. No part of this publication may be reproduced in whole or in part, or stored in a retrieval system, or transmitted in any form or by any means, electronic, mechanical, photocopying, recording, or otherwise, without written permission of the publisher

Library of Congress Cataloging-in-Publication Data
Names: Meister, Cari, author. | Capstone Press.
Title: The electoral college : a kid's guide / by Cari Meister.
Description: North Mankato, Minnesota : Capstone Press a Capstone imprint, 2020. | Series: Kids' guide to elections | Series: Fact Finders | "Captivate is published by Capstone Press, an imprint of Capstone"—T.p. verso. | Includes webography. | Includes index. | Audience: Ages 8-11 years (provided by Capstone Press) |
Identifiers: LCCN 2019048322 (print) | LCCN 2019048323 (ebook) | ISBN 9781543591422 (eBook PDF) | ISBN 9781543591385 (Library Binding) | ISBN 9781496666024 (Paperback)
Subjects: LCSH: Electoral college—United States—History—Juvenile literature. | Elections—United States—History—Juvenile literature. | Presidents—United States—Election—Juvenile literature. | Politics, Practical—United States—Juvenile literature. | United States—Politics and government—Juvenile literature.
Classification: LCC JK529 (ebook) | LCC JK529 .M45 2020 (print) | DDC 324.6/3—dc23
LC record available at https://lccn.loc.gov/2019048322
Summary: Gives facts about the Electoral College and how it's part of U.S. elections.

Image Credits
Alamy: Bob Daemmrich, 20, Ian Dagnall, 7, (top), pawlopicasso, 17; AP Images: Zach Gibson, 26; Newscom: CQ Roll Call/Tom Williams, 13, 14, Jeff Malet Photography, 22, Joseph Sohm, 25, Polaris/Sam Simmonds, 18, Reuters/Brendan McDermid, 24, Reuters/Jim Bourg, 12, Reuters/Rebecca Cook, 23; Shutterstock: amadeustx, 5, Andy Dune, 15, Bardocz Peter, 11 (countries), DNetromphotos, 16, Everett - Art, 7, (Washington, Adams, Madison), Everett Historical, 7, (Jefferson), Giraphics, Cover, mark reinstein, 10, Monkey Business Images, 29, Nicholas Martinson, 4, Paul Boucher, 27, PyTy, 11 (world map), Rob Crandall, 8-9, txking, 19

Design Elements
Capstone; Shutterstock: openeyed

Editorial Credits
Editor: Michelle Parkin; Designer: Bobbie Nuytten;
Media Researcher: Jo Miller; Production Specialist: Laura Manthe

All internet sites appearing in back matter were available and accurate when this book was sent to press.

Table of Contents

Say What? 4

The History Behind the Electoral College 6

Winning By the Numbers 12

How Does It Work? 18

Pros and Cons 22

What Is Your Role? 28

    Glossary 30
    Read More 31
    Internet Sites 31
    Index 32

Glossary terms are **bold** on first use.

Say What?

There's always a lot of buzz when it's time to elect a new president. There should be! Being the leader of our country is a big job. It is our duty as **citizens** to vote for who we think will do the best job.

Four U.S. presidents are carved into Mount Rushmore.

The president's desk is in the Oval Office at the White House.

But did you know that votes alone don't choose a president? When the election is over, a smaller group of people meet to name the winner. This is called the Electoral College.

The Electoral College is not a place. It is a process that our country has used since the first election for president.

How does the Electoral College work? Why do we have it? Is this a good way to elect our leader? Let's take a closer look.

FACT: George Washington was America's first president. He was elected in 1789.

The History Behind the Electoral College

The Electoral College is written in the **U.S. Constitution**. When our leaders wrote the Constitution, they had different ideas about how the president should be chosen. They knew they didn't want someone to be born into the job, like a king or queen.

Some wanted the U.S. **Congress** to pick the president. But this meant that citizens would not be able to decide who the president would be. Others thought the people should elect our leader. The person who got the most votes would win. But states that had higher **populations** would have more power than states with fewer people.

The U.S. Constitution was written by a group of men called the Founding Fathers.

In the end, our early leaders created the Electoral College. It gave some power to every state in America. This way, citizens in smaller states still had a say in their government. The Electoral College is still used today.

FACT: Four of the men who helped write the Constitution became U.S. presidents.

George Washington John Adams James Madison Thomas Jefferson

A True Democracy?

Many people believe that the United States is a direct **democracy**. That's not really true. In a direct democracy, the **majority** of people make the decisions. This means that more than half of a group needs to vote for the idea for it to pass.

Let's look at an example. Imagine a farmer lives on a large piece of land. Leaders would like to build a road through this land. The farmer does not want to sell. All the people in town vote. Most people vote to build the road.

The farmer didn't give up the land. But the farmer still loses. In this type of democracy, a person's **rights** can be changed or taken away. Our government doesn't work like this.

In the U.S., government decisions are not made by a majority vote.

Our early leaders believed in a person's rights. Because of this, our government is called a representative republic. People choose leaders to be part of our government. These leaders make decisions for us and our country. This means everyone gets a say, not just most people.

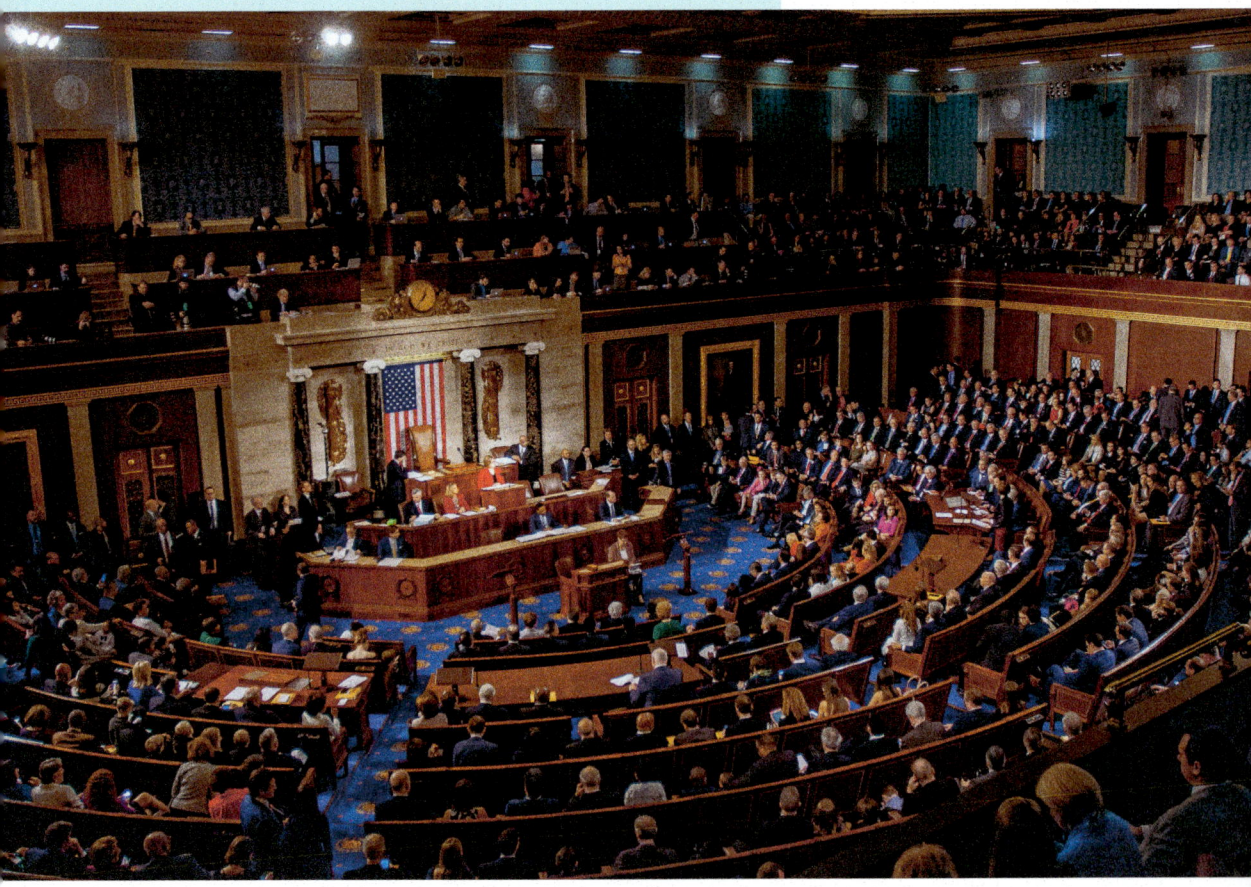

Members of Congress represent citizens across the country.

REPRESENTATIVE REPUBLICS AROUND THE WORLD

Three countries around the world are considered representative republics.

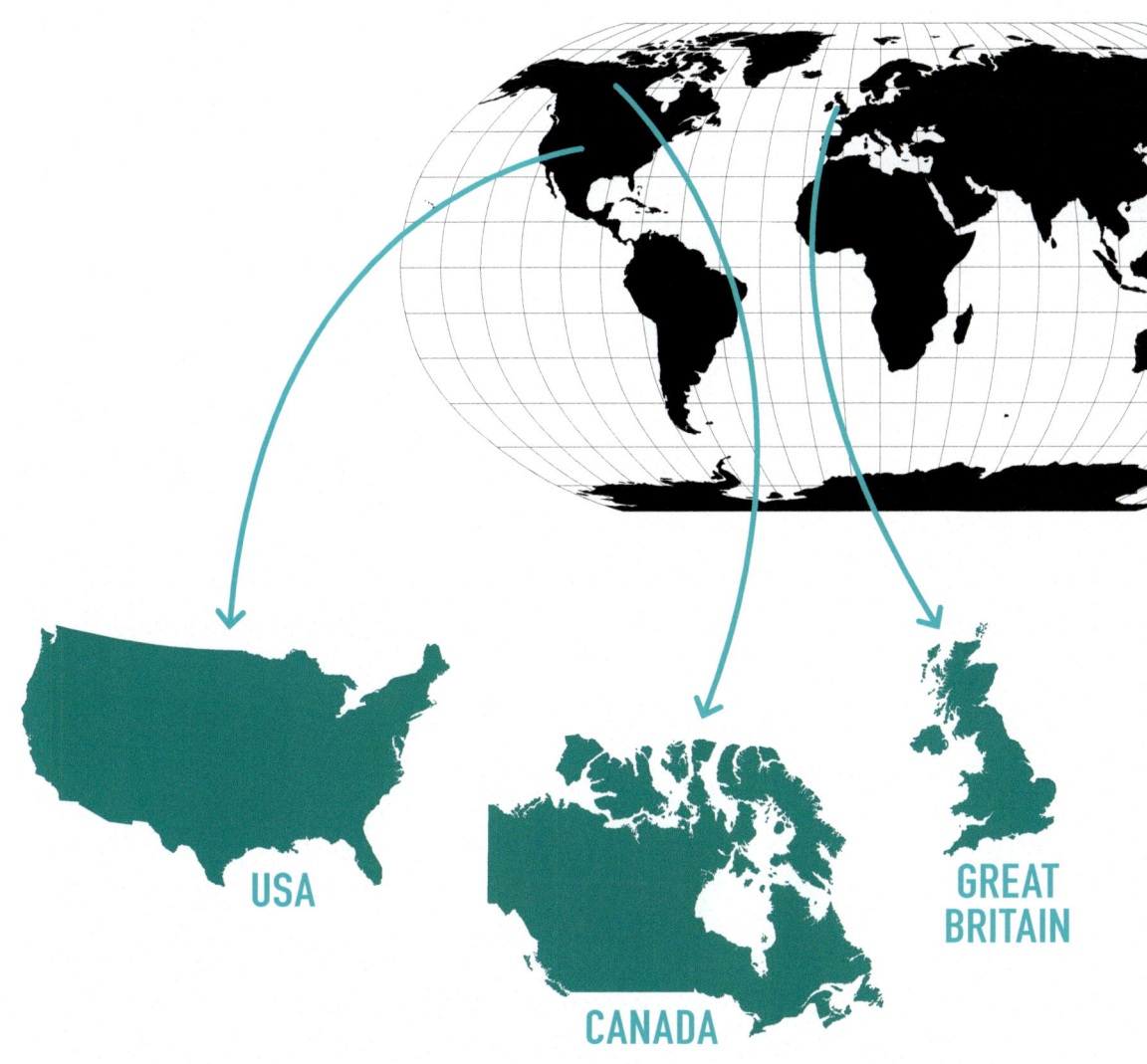

Winning by the Numbers

A person who is running in an election is called a **candidate**. A candidate needs to win the **general election** to become president. The general election happens every four years. The candidate with the most **electoral votes** wins.

Barack Obama (left) became president after winning the general election in 2008.

Electors vote for the president. They are chosen by the people in their states. Each elector gets one vote.

FACT: People who are already working in the government cannot be electors. This includes senators and representatives.

Electoral votes are kept inside ballot boxes until they are ready to be counted.

Each state gets a certain number of electoral votes. This is decided by the number of members it has in Congress. Every state gets two senators. But the number of representatives is based on the state's population. States with fewer people have fewer representatives. This means these states don't have as many electoral votes as states with a lot of people.

Senators Rand Paul (left) and Mitch McConnell represent Kentucky.

There are a total of 538 electors. Why 538? This is the total number of senators, representatives, and electors from Washington, D.C. Here's how the math works out:

 **100 SENATORS**

 **435 HOUSE REPRESENTATIVES**

 **3 ELECTORS FROM WASHINGTON, D.C.**

 **538 ELECTORAL VOTES**

The state of Minnesota has a population of about 5.6 million people. The state has two senators and eight representatives. Add the number of senators and representatives together. Minnesota gets 10 electoral votes.

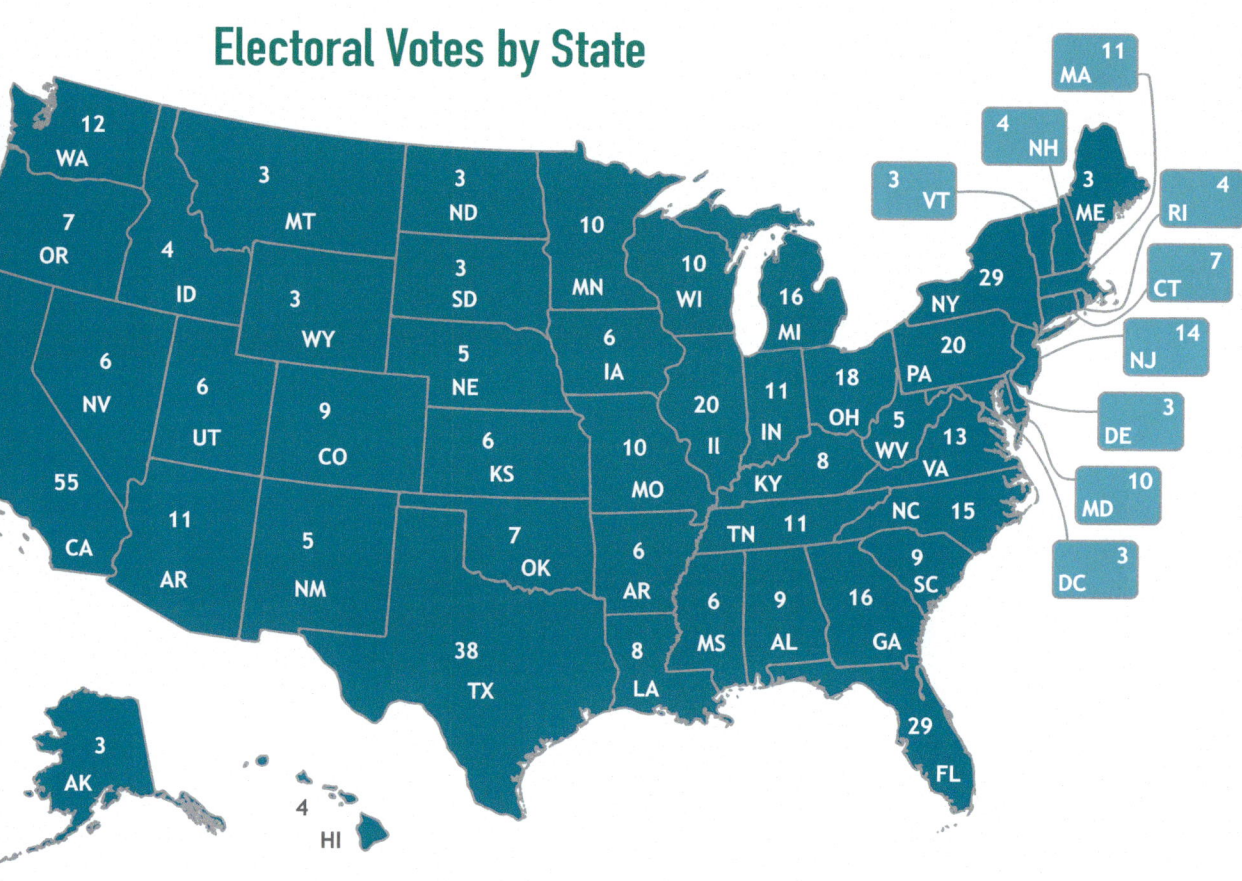

Electoral Votes by State

That may seem like a lot of people. But let's look at the state of California. Almost 40 million people live in California. The state has two senators and 53 representatives. This means California gets 55 electoral votes.

Now let's look at the state of Wyoming. This state has two senators and one representative. It gets three electoral votes. Why only three? Compared to larger states, Wyoming has a lower population. It has about 578,000 people.

Hollywood Boulevard in Los Angeles, California

How Does It Work?

On Election Day, people vote for their favorite candidate. Then the votes are counted. TV programs across the country keep track of the results. The candidate who gets the most votes in a state is the winner of that state. All of the state's electoral votes go to that candidate.

Supporters of Hillary Clinton watched the presidential election results in 2016.

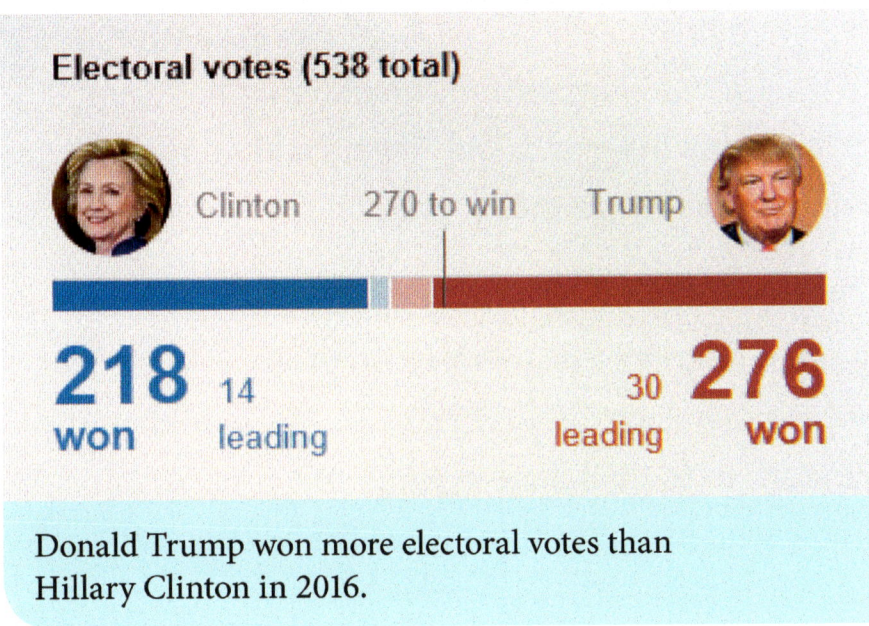

Donald Trump won more electoral votes than Hillary Clinton in 2016.

There are only two states that divide up their electoral votes. In Maine and Nebraska, the overall winner gets two of the state's electoral votes. But then the winner in each **district** gets one electoral vote. Each district may have a different winner.

WHO GETS TO VOTE?

A person must be at least 18 years old to vote for president. He or she must also be a U.S. citizen.

A candidate needs at least 271 electoral votes to become president. After this number has been reached, a winner is called. Voters will know who will serve as the next U.S. president.

State electors can be chosen before or after the general election. Electors have to promise to vote for the person who won in their state. In December, the electors go to their state capitols and vote. We already know who won. But this makes the election official.

An elector turns in her vote at Texas's state capitol.

THE POPULAR VOTE

The **popular vote** is how most of the people voted. A candidate who gets the most votes across the country wins the popular vote. Most times, the person who becomes president also wins the popular vote. But that is not always the case. So far five presidents have lost the popular vote but still won the election.

- John Quincy Adams was elected president in 1824. He lost the popular vote to Andrew Jackson.

- Rutherford B. Hayes was elected president in 1876. He lost the popular vote to Samuel Tilden.

- Benjamin Harrison was elected president in 1888. He lost the popular vote to Grover Cleveland, who had just served as president.

- George W. Bush was elected president in 2000. He lost the popular vote to Al Gore, who had just served as vice president.

- Donald Trump was elected president in 2016. He lost the popular vote to former senator and former first lady Hillary Clinton.

Pros and Cons

Keeping the Electoral College

People have talked about the Electoral College for years. Some think it's an important part of picking our leaders. By using the Electoral College, people living in smaller states have a say in the election. Their concerns are heard. If it was removed, candidates running for president wouldn't travel to smaller states.

a protestor against the Electoral College

The Electoral College also helps when votes need to be recounted. Sometimes election results are very close in a state. A candidate can ask for the votes to be counted again. Because of the Electoral College, only that state's votes would need to be recounted. We don't have to recount the votes in the whole country.

Also, a candidate must get votes from people all over the U.S. to win. This means a candidate can't spend all his or her time in one part of the country.

People against the Electoral College held signs in front of Michigan's state capitol in 2016.

Against the Electoral College

Some people think we should get rid of the Electoral College. They argue it is too old and confusing. But what should it be replaced with? Many believe that the president should be elected by the popular vote. In fact, 14 states have decided to give their electoral votes to the winner of the popular vote—no matter who wins in their state.

Other people feel that their votes don't count in an election. They are not actually voting for president, the electors are. This can lead to fewer people voting.

Not as many people voted in the 2016 presidential election compared to 2012.

Also, electors promise to vote the same way their state does. But there are no laws forcing them. Some electors have broken their word. They gave their state's electoral votes to a different candidate.

Senators Roy Blunt (left) and Amy Klobuchar (right) review electoral college votes for president in 2017.

There are many sides to this argument. But for now, the Electoral College will stay a part of the election. But this may change in the future. In 2019 at least three people running for president wanted to get rid of the Electoral College.

In 2019 Senator Elizabeth Warren spoke to a crowd about removing the Electoral College.

What Is Your Role?

You may not be able to vote in the next election. But you still have a job to do! Learn as much as you can about the election. Watch the candidates on TV and online. Find out what they stand for. Do you agree with what they are saying?

Talk to your family and friends about what issues matter to them. Ask them what they think about the Electoral College. If they aren't sure what it is, let them know! Look online to see how people in other states feel about the Electoral College.

Learning about the Electoral College now is important. It will help you become an educated voter when it's time for you to vote!

Take part in discussions about the candidates and the Electoral College.

GET OUT THE VOTE

What is the most important thing a voter can do? Vote! It is how our government hears our issues and concerns. It is our duty as citizens. But not all people decide to vote. So get the word out. Talk to people you know. Ask them if they are going to vote. If they say no, encourage them to vote and make their voices heard.

Glossary

candidate (KAN-duh-dayt)—a person who runs for office, such as president

citizen (SI-tuh-zuhn)—a member of a country or state who has a right to live there

Congress (KAHN-gruhs)—the part of the government that makes laws; Congress includes the Senate and the House of Representatives

Constitution (kon-stuh-TOO-shun)—a written system of laws that states the rights of people and powers of government

democracy (di-MAH-kruh-see)—a form of government where the people can choose their leaders

district (DIS-trikt)—an area with a certain number of voters

elector (i-LEK-tohr)—a person who votes to choose between two or more people running for office

general election (JEN-ur-uhl i-LEK-shuhn)—an election that is held in all the states at the same time

population (pop-yuh-LAY-shuhn)—the number of people who live in an area

popular vote (POP-yuh-lur VOHT)—the number of people who vote for a candidate

right (RITE)—something that the law says you can have or do

Read More

Edwards, Sue Bradford. *The Electoral College Series: Debating the Issues.* New York: AV2 by Weigl, 2019.

Gunderson, Jessica. *Understanding Your Role in Elections.* North Mankato, MN: Capstone Press, 2018.

Hunt, Santana. *What Is the Electoral College?* New York: Gareth Stevens Publishing, 2018.

Internet Sites

What Is an Election?
https://www.dkfindout.com/us/more-find-out/what-does-politician-do/what-is-an-election/

How Does Someone Become the President?
https://www.usa.gov/election#item-212481

U.S. Government, Electoral College
https://www.ducksters.com/history/us_government/electoral_college.php

Index

candidates, 12, 18, 20, 22, 23, 26, 28
elections, 5, 12, 22, 23, 24, 27, 28
　general elections, 12, 20
electoral votes, 12, 14, 16, 17, 18, 19, 20, 24, 26
electors, 13, 15, 20, 24, 26
presidents, 4, 5, 6, 12, 13, 20, 22, 24, 27
representative republics, 10–11
rights, 9, 10
states, 6, 7, 13, 14, 16, 17, 18, 19, 20, 23, 24, 26, 28

U.S. Congress, 6, 14
　representatives, 14, 15, 16, 17
　senators, 14, 15, 16, 17
U.S. Constitution, 6
voting, 4, 5, 6, 8, 13, 18, 20, 23, 24, 26, 28